REFLECTIONS ON FREEDOM

A Manifesto for My People, the Human Beings

J.D. Bradley

ISBN: 0-9888-1800-0
ISBN-13: 9780988818002

Cover design by: MJCimageworks
Library of Congress Control Number: 2018675309
Printed in the United States of America

To the good people of the world

THE GRAND ILLUSION

Everything in the world is much different than we have been conditioned to believe. There are people that rule us and think of us as cattle, and send us to war against each other, and manipulate our minds into thinking insane things; like one race is better than another, or people that believe in a different god than you should die, but the great awakening has begun.

The people at the top, who parasitically take the best that life has to offer from us, while only leaving us table scraps that we savagely fight each other for, have so warped the human experience as to have practically removed the concept of truth from mankind. The general populace lives in a life of confused lies which have been thrust upon them and have no basis to judge what is real and what is not. They are rightfully angry but unable to focus that hatred at those who oppress us. Up is down;

Left is right. Our general populace believes that "WAR IS PEACE, FREEDOM IS SLAVERY, and IGNORANCE IS STRENGTH!", as George Orwell prophetically proclaimed. We have otherwise intelligent young adults who believe that socialism will set them free. They champion their/our enslavement as it is some desirous prize, and proudly extoll its virtue. We are so far removed from what we the human beings should be experiencing. It's time for a real change. It is upon us.

Our perceptions have been very carefully manipulated since birth to deny us awareness of the political realities of the world.

The great awakening began years ago. I roused from my slumber two decades ago. Early in my awakening I was scoffed at by somnambulists, but today we are multiplying exponentially. Mathematics itself is on our side. Soon we will be one collective boot that will stomp down on our very few oppressors. We will be unstoppable.

The truth is especially painful to accept because it's been kept from us our whole lives. The truth is nevertheless the truth. There's nothing more important.

A vote for a Democrat Presidential candidate is a vote for totalitarianism and general enslavement. A vote for a Republican Presidential candidate is a vote for totalitarianism and general enslavement.

That is how distorted the system has become; both candidates on a Federal level are the candidates of Goldman Sachs, et al and will pursue the agenda of their superiors at the expense of the common man.

The banks are fucking our lives up.

The willingly ignorant will receive whatever fate befalls them and have no idea of freedom.

Only the perverse experience joy from subjugating their fellow human beings and deserve only eradication.

Socialism is just another plan to keep us enslaved. The same bankers that own us, own that camp, too. The Bolshevik Revolution was financed by Wall Street. How many millions of people died to make that check mark in their asset column? Those were millions of people that mattered and had other people that loved them, who might have been executed also. That is unacceptable.

Our slavery is so pervasive that almost no one questions it.

The most horrible thing about our current societal model is that it is a "zero sum game", which is rigged against us. It doesn't have to be that way at all. There is no need for poverty, but in their minds "It is not enough that we be rich, but you must also be poor."

The Great Depression was the so called "Federal" "Reserve" (It is neither federal nor a reserve) test driving their power and plundering the land. The suffering of the common man was immaterial. In their minds, we are cattle. How does that make you feel? It makes me very, very angry.

Our active duty troops are not "Protecting Our Freedoms!" The equation is much more sophisticated than that, and they're not at all "protecting our freedoms". In reality, they are unwitting pawns fighting to oppress and terrorize and kill people in other countries on behalf of the banks and corporations. I was one of them once and I had no idea of my servitude on behalf of evil. Someday soon they may be turned against us, but I suspect most of them will refuse to kill us and join our side, as most of them have noble hearts.

We are at war. Most on our side do not realize it so far but that is rapidly changing.

Currently, society is a huge, complex lie, and we all suffer because of its Machiavellian machinations. Ultimately its purpose is to perpetuate our enslavement for the enrichment of the parasite class. We are beginning to rouse from our slumber, slowly at first, but the number of the awakened is exploding.

The world is a trap for your mind to fall into, to prevent free thought. It has been designed to subjugate us. Too bad for its designers that more of us rouse each day. It's ultimately going to be a fight of our numbers versus their stolen wealth. There are over eight billion of us and just hundreds of them, minus their servants who will eventually be swayed to our side. We have already won in the future.

Our education system has been purposefully diluted. If the powers that be wanted to create critically thinking, caring individuals, we would teach critical thinking, personal finance and ethics, among other things. Clearly the powers that be do not want you to be able to exercise your faculties. Why might that be?

"It is well enough that people of the nation do not understand our banking and monetary system, for if they did, I believe there would be a revolution before tomorrow morning." Henry Ford

We are waking up. The "red pill" is being taken on a global scale. Even Zbigniew Brezisnki has admitted this (much to his chagrin). There has been in his words, "A massive, global, political awakening". They went too far with 9-11, and their arrogance betrayed them. (Btw, the "Official Story" is a complete farce. For beginners, please Google "dancing Israelis"). We didn't even know we were at war. How fucked up is that? We know now, and more know every day. They are powerful, but we are many.

RACISM

I hereby declare that racism is destructive idiocy and that we need to cease to participation in it.

I do not believe in racism. I find it heinous and vitriolic. I feel it is a trap to keep us down by pitting us against each other. My specific people, the Irish, the so called "niggers of Europe" toiled alongside the African slaves for over 200 years. I don't have patience for that kind of hatred, and it makes me angry. The very concept of slavery offends me. How can one human do that to another? We are all one people with a common enemy.

If you are racist, I oppose you. I oppose irrational hatred against other human beings.

The truest treason to humanity is the attempted and/or actual enslavement of one's fellow human beings. The most appropriate punishment for that behavior is death by prolonged torture.

At no time in human history has racism been

a benevolent force. At no time has it furthered our interests as human beings. Its elimination will benefit everyone except those who exploit it to keep us fighting against each other instead of against them.

Until you can learn to love your brothers and sisters, as your brothers and sisters, you will always remain in chains.

I do not hate you because of some primitive belief system that says I have to. I feel we have been pitted against each other in order to hold all of us down. I hope we can join together and move both of our interests forward. If you subscribe to racism, you subscribe to your own enslavement and mine also.

When all my brothers and sisters across the world recognize each other as brothers and sisters of one race, the human race, "The Man" will concede.

Just as in a penal system, our current society is designed to pit the varying races against each other, in order to keep them from uniting and creating a perfect life, or some semblance thereof.

My people are the human beings and my enemies are those who divide and enslave us.

The ugly truth about racism is that there's a racist group in charge of everything and use racism to keep us down, fighting among ourselves, divided, when we should be one. We are all human beings and I love all of us, except those who oppress us. Read and educate yourself, and I promise I'll fight beside you no matter your race, because we are one people. Oh, plus if you point out their evil, they accuse you of being racist. How clever is that? Most people believe them, because television says so.

How can you be proud to be your race? Be proud of your humanity.

Join hands, my brothers and sisters, and let's truly be free for the first time in history. Racism is my people, being pitted against each other, in ignorance, to preserve the status quo, which enslaves us. My people are the human beings and we will be free. We will demand freedom and then take it.

ZIONISTS

Firstly, I want to emphatically state that I have no problem with Jews, or any other race for that matter. I am not anti-Jewish in even a small degree. I am 100% pro-human. I cannot imagine a world without the Jewish people. They have had a profound influence in the history of the world, and many people that I admire greatly, i.e., Noam Chomsky, Carl Sagan, Shlomo Sand, and Norman Finkelstein for instance, are Jewish; that being said, there is a minority of racists among them that that are wreaking havoc in our world, the first and foremost being the Rothschild family and their megalomaniacal ilk, and they've been doing it for centuries. They have to be obliterated if we are ever to be free. I advocate their destruction.

"Money has no motherland; financiers are without patriotism and without decency; their sole object is gain."

- Napoleon Bonaparte

Not all Jewish people are Zionists and not all

Zionists are Jewish, but 100% of Zionists are actively involved in our enslavement. Blame the Zionists, not "the Jews". Blaming "the Jews" is not only wrong from a logical standpoint, and unfair to the innocent, but is a trap that too many well intentioned people have fallen into so that they can be branded "anti-Semites", which ends a very important discussion.

Anyone who points out the evils of the Zionists is branded an "anti-Semite", as likely I will be. I have no problems with the Jewish people at large as I consider all human beings my brothers and sisters. If you are Jewish and expose the evils of the Zionists, the racist Jews (the Zionists) brand you as a "self-loathing Jew". In reality, you are a quality human being, deserving much respect for your valor.

"Give me control of a nation's money and I care not who makes the laws." Mayer Amschel Bauer (Rothschild)

Zionism is humanity's most dangerous enemy. It has subjugated us. It has exploited us. It has turned us against each other in order to hold us down. It is well thought out and actively enforced. It is doomed when enough of us wake up. The absolute evil it has accomplished almost defies description. It has caused two world wars so far and is itching for a third. These are people who send us to die, but who are too cowardly to fight themselves.

"It is untrue that I or anyone else in Germany wanted war in 1939. It was wanted and provoked solely by international statesmen either of Jewish origin or working for Jewish interests. Nor had I ever wished that after the appalling First World War, there would ever be a second against either England or America."—Adolf Hitler, April 1945.

"Every time we do something, you tell me America will do this and will do that…I want to tell you something very clear: Don't worry about American pressure on Israel. We, the Jewish people, control America, and the Americans know it." Ariel Sharon, Israel's 11th Prime Minister October 3, 2001. I believe he was referring to the politicians in D.C., not the American public, who so far mostly hasn't the knowledge of the Zionists dominating our country because they own the mass media and Hollywood.

Zionism is simply Jewish supremacism. It's much more than a philosophy desiring a homeland for the Jewish people. I'm against any racist supremacism, including white supremacism. It is all destructive, but the atrocities perpetrated by Zionism dwarf the evils of all the others.

"We shall have world government, whether or not we like it. The only question is whether world government will be achieved by conquest or consent." James Paul Warburg, foreign agent for the Rothschild dynasty.

The truth is found in history but distorted by the mass media which serves to enslave our minds. The Rothschilds and their ilk have been controlling everything to detriment to us all for centuries. The trans-Atlantic slave trade was 100% racist-Jewish (Zionist, but at the time that term did not exist) owned. For over 200 years, the Irish and the African slaves worked side by side. Both the Armenian and Ukrainian holocausts were at the hands of racist (Zionist) Jews. Very likely, what you believe about "the holocaust" is not true. It is the most powerful lie ever told to justify the invasion of Palestine and the genocide of the beautiful Palestinian people, who had done nothing to offend. The slave labor camps in Germany were used to support the war and the obliteration of its inmates would have worked against the German war machine. The emaciated bodies you've seen were the result of supply lines being bombed out of existence, typhus, and the piles of bodies were the German victims of the Dresden firebombing. Both the Zionist owned media and the Zionist owned Hollywood have made that last simple truth unimaginable for almost everyone. I understand what a shocking statement that is, as it was once shocking to me. Please do not confuse Jewish with Zionist, and please search for the truth. Truth fears NO investigation.

"Since I entered politics, I have chiefly had men's views confided to me privately. Some of the biggest men in the United States, in the fields of commerce and manufacturing, are afraid of somebody. They know that there is a power somewhere so organized, so subtle, so watchful, so interlocked, so complete, so pervasive, that they had better not speak above their breath when they speak in condemnation of it." President Woodrow Wilson, punk assed bitch and sitting President when the so called "Federal" "Reserve" was granted charter.

It is a little known fact that the Zionists and the Nazis worked together early in Hitler's administration to help German Jews to immigrate to Palestine. Their program was called the "Haavara Agreement". The Jewish people who did not want to relocate were sacrificed to the German concentration (work) camps by said Zionists as pawns to generate outrage by the world and pave the way to the ultimate invasion of Palestine and the establishment of a Jewish state of Israel. The Palestinian people refer to this invasion as the "Nakba", or catastrophe. It was, and continues to be, their holocaust.

It is a cowardly people that declare war without the goddamned common courtesy to warn their adversaries.

Our government was long ago coopted by the foreign government of Israel. Our economy was long ago enslaved by the Rothschild family and their co-conspirators. They accomplished this by deception and the absolute lack of balls and common courtesy that it takes to wage war without declaring their intent. The last American President that stood up to them was Kennedy. You remember what they did to him, right? The one before that was Lincoln. Do you suppose that is a coincidence?

For the uninitiated: World War Two was a war between two banking systems, one much like our own American Revolution (the Germans being that side) and the other, the slaves of the Rothschilds (the Allies). The Germans had discovered a way to be prosperous, which is the natural condition for a society without the shackles of the "Central Bank System", as had the Japanese. Look into the "German economic miracle".

All Jewish Zionists and almost every Jew in Israel are Ashkenazi Jews. Ashkenazi Jews, by the way are not the same "Jews" from the bible. They are Khazar converts and they're the ones literally killing the family of Jesus (the modern Palestinians are his descendants). I'm not even Christian, and this disgusts me. Ethiopian Jews are treated as second class citizens in Israel by Ashkenazi, and their women have been sterilized by the State, without their foreknowledge of what was about to happen to them. How crazy is Jew on Jew racism especially when you consider the Talmud, which serves as a guide to render harmless, and enslave other cultures?

The reason our government kisses Zionist ass so

much is that have been secretly organized, for generations, to subdue everyone else.

The Great Depression was a big, big experiment with the power that they had acquired through the creation of the so called “Federal” “Reserve” and they pulled it off. Flash forward to 9-11. They thought it was going to be just as easy and no one would figure it out. Their mistake. Bastards. The situation is just that simple. When Israel, along with elements of our own government (which Israel controls) perpetrated 9-11, a lot of people began to rouse from their slumber and their ultimate demise was placed in motion.

Investigate “Eisenhower’s death camps”. That’s how to do genocide. (Covered very well in “Other Losses” by James Bacque)

How many levels of monsters are there at this world? We have serial killers and sexual predators that are clearly monsters, but they can only victimize individuals. Worse than them, we have Rothschilds and the other banksters that victimize humanity itself.

No Rothschild has ever had to worry how they were going to feed their children. They have never worried about where their next meal was coming from. They have never lost a job or been evicted. They have likely never been assaulted (as much as they deserve it). Yet, they created this system where we have to worry about and experience these things so that they do not. Do you see what has to happen? Their cohort families have to go also. Everyone who was involved in our enslavement has to be punished. Thus begins the Age of Aquarius.

The ultimate tools of oppression the Zionists have available to them are the central banks of the world (ours being the so-called "Federal" "Reserve") and their "taxing" agencies (the Internal Revenue Service) which are simply enforcement agencies for the central banks. They control the very economy. From there, their power only multiplies. Both need to be discarded to the trashcan of history. The economies of the world, and humanity itself, will flourish with their demise.

"100% of what is collected is absorbed solely by interest on the Federal Debt...all individual income tax revenues are gone before one nickel is spent on the services taxpayers expect from government." From the Grace Commission report, submitted to President Ronald Reagan

The control over society desired by the top Zionists eclipses all of their previous horrific behavior. Their desire is to implement slavery to such a degree as to dwarf the dystopianism of Orwell's 1984. They are not playing around. I do feel them to be doomed, but that's what it is. That's how serious things are.

"For we are opposed around the world by a monolithic and ruthless conspiracy that replies primarily on covert means for expanding its sphere of influence, on infiltration instead of invasion, on subversion instead of elections, on intimidation instead of free choice, on guerrillas by night instead of armies by day. It is a system which has conscripted vast human and material resources into the building of a tightly knit, highly efficient machine that combines military, diplomatic, intelligence, economic, scientific, and political operations.

Its preparations are concealed, not published. Its mistakes are buried, not headlined. Its dissenters are silenced, not praised. No expenditure is questioned, no rumor is printer, no secret is revealed." President John Fitzgerald Kennedy months before they had him assassinated.

"Anti-Semitism" [an-tee-sem-i-tiz-uh m]

Noun

1) The very natural anger and indignation that arises in response to the belligerent and racist attitudes and actions of the non-Semitic racist Ashkenazi fake "Jews"

2) A Jedi mindfuck trick used to deflect blame for bullshit, racist behavior onto the victim and protect the perpetrators of said evil.

3) An emotional manipulation phrase used to shut down rational discourse.

And while we're on the subject... "The Holocaust" is mathematically impossible. Open your mind. We have been lied to our whole lives.

The first killing operations allegedly began at Chelmno concentration camp in occupied Poland December 8, 1941 and the last concentration to be liberated was on May 9, 1945. This gives us 1,247 days of "genocide". I'm not even going to factor in that the other concentration camps opened later and the closed at different times which would give the Germans less opportunity to allegedly kill Jews. We are going to run on the assumption that ALL concentration camps ran at peak efficiency from December 8, 1941 to May 9, 1945. In 1,247 days, it is claimed that 6,000,000 Jews were killed, and their remains destroyed. That would mean that 4,812 prisoners were killed every single day during that time, AND their remains were disposed of.

Since there are 24 hours in a day, that means 200 prisoners an hour were killed non-stop for almost 3 and a half years, which is also 3.34 a minute, every minute, non-stop for the duration of that time. Imagine the resources and logistics needed to pull off such a monstrous deed. That's more than one person killed, and their remains disposed of every 20 seconds, 24 hours a day for almost 3 and a half years. Now, factor in the fact that Germany was fighting a two front war the same time against opponents that were not wasting such resources. The laws of physical reality make this impossible... and that doesn't even count the non-Jews allegedly killed in the concentration camps.

Allegedly there were 5 million non-Jews killed at the concentration camps, for a grand total of 11 million victims. Let's do the math again...11 million people in 1,247 days comes to 8,821 victims a day, or 367 an hour, or 6.1 a minute, or slightly more than one person killed EVERY TEN SECONDS, AND THEIR REMAINS DISPOSED OF FOR ALMOST THREE AND A HALF YEARS, while Germany was fighting a two front war against enemies that weren't wasting such vast resources. That is a physical impossibility.

Does anyone really think that scenario is realistic? Perhaps we should reinvestigate to get the truth.

I'm not denying the existence of concentration camps, just the narrative that has been sold to us. The numbers don't add up. If the narrative was real, it would stand up to scrutiny.

They were slave camps used to further the war effort, just as we had Japanese internment camps in this country, and that is also, very, very wrong, but we have been sold this story to justify the "Nakba" or invasion of Palestine and subjugation of its people and the theft of their land, which is insane because the Palestinian people had nothing to do with the so called "holocaust". The emaciated prisoners were starved because the supply lines had been bombed out of existence by the allies, and the stacks of bodies were bodies of German civilians killed in the firebombing of Dresden. A more evil plot defies the imagination.

Now, factor in that the memoirs of FDR, Churchill, AND Stalin didn't mention "the holocaust" and that a very real genocide had already been accomplished by Zionists in the Ukraine. Look up the Holodomor. Why do you suppose we never hear about it? How about the approximately 60,000,000 Soviets killed over time by the same faction?

TELEVISION AND THE MASS MEDIA

The world that we have been led to believe that we live in is largely an artificial construct, designed to control our minds and limit our ability to be sentient. You are likely a slave to masters that control your thoughts, to a very large degree. Mainstream media is a weapon that is used to oppress us and our thought processes; to control our minds. It is Zionist owned and another tool to keep us enslaved.

The mass media's purpose is not to inform and educate but to confound and control what we think. Any adherent to Rush Limbaugh or Hannity or whomthefuckever has no idea what's going on in the world. CNN/FOX News are simply the state sanctioned propaganda channels.

Mainstream media exists to confuse us and tell us to choose horrible options which will lead to disastrous consequences for us, but further enrich the ruling class who own said media. There is NO truth to be found there, only victimization. If you form your opinions from the nightly news or your local newspaper, you are a mind control victim. Please move away from that and towards truth. Join us outside of the "Matrix".

"LOOK, STUPID PEOPLE, THE DOMINANT CLASS IS PRETENDING TO CARE ABOUT YOU WHILE THEY SELL OUT THE FUTURE OF YOUR GRANDCHILDREN...and everything is okay..." the mass media. Why do people accept that? Well primarily because we have been conditioned to.

When I absolutely have no value for someone's uneducated opinion, I tell them to go watch television.

Move away from television. Do things that are worthwhile instead.

The media circus that surrounds inflammatory issues is a tool to keep truth suppressed.

Mainstream media pundits should all suffer horrible deaths. There is no ample punishment for the evil that they promote. "SLEEP PEOPLE!!!" The Man.

"Do you ever wonder why they call it television "PROGRAMMING"?" Unknown free thinker. I want to attribute it to George Carlin but have failed to verify that. Saint George.

Hollywood is a major power in both its ability to raise capital and control our minds.

"Criticism of television is anti-Semitism!" The Man.

All the important secrets can be found in World War II. Why do you suppose that's almost all that shows on the so-called "History Channel"? Your minds must be controlled about WWII. Hitler, the so-called "Ultimate Evil" was nothing of the sort. What if you've been lied to your whole life about everything about the "good war"? Could you accept that? What if it was not a good war? Because it was not.

When those who manipulate us decide to exploit a racial incident, they skew the facts in order to cause the maximum amount of fallout possible and make us angry at each other. Don't fall for that bullshit. We are all one people. We all have a common enemy.

It is a relaxed mind that watches too much television, as in it can't do a mental pushup.

Hollywood is waging a war against our minds and has gotten phenomenally rich doing so.

So called reality television simply instructs its naive audience to behave ignorantly. It is nothing more than ignorant people doing ignorant things for an ignorant and impressionable audience. Why do people watch it? I suppose, because they are ignorant. Some of them got pulled down to ignorance by television, some were born ignorant. “Reality” television is a guide to how to be a colossal fuck up.

I don’t think that very many people understand the influence that mass media and advertising, understand how mind control works. They’re not supposed to. That’s by design. They are a product to be purchased and sold. We all are, but some of us notice.

Television is a hypnotic weapon aimed at your mind, designed to control your opinions and tell you what to do. Unplug television from your life. Realize that Hollywood is the Kingdom of Lies.

Television is a terrible drug. Remove yourself from its programming. Take up boxing, or some such thing. Become dangerous. Read.

Never trust the media; allow it but recognize its bias.

I have nothing but disdain for television in case you had not noticed.

Imagine the social ramifications when most people willingly line up and take shots of dubious value into their arms because television and other media propaganda tools like newspapers and magazines told them that that is a good thing to do.

Hollywood's premier product is mind control. Entertainment is secondary.

Fuck television. Fuck Hollywood. Fuck the mainstream media. Read a goddamned book. Educate yourself and prosper.

RELIGION

... So the son of god, who is god, planned his own crucifixion to save us from our sins, that he created to begin with, and sacrificed his life even though he knew he would be resurrected, so he didn't really sacrifice his life ... tell me a fucking fairy tale. I sincerely care for a lot of people that believe this nonsense, but clearly, IT IS NONSENSE! The true creator, which we have little conception of, gave us logic which refutes this bullshit!

The bad news, at least for superstitious people, is that there is no Christian god. The good news is that once we realize this, as a society, we can take charge of ourselves and make good decisions which will benefit us all. I am not, however saying there's no god, just that we are incapable of defining it and have no business trying to set up rules for it. All we can do is listen to our hearts and minds.

Religion is bullshit about bullshit being presented to you by someone who has either been tricked by bullshit, or exploits the bullshit, in order to trick you into being foolish and doing bullshit things. My apologies to my Christian friends- I never say any rude shit on your religious posts on Facebook because I care about you but this is how I feel.

I'm not part of any organized religion and I don't believe in what they say. It's fine with me if those people that go to church believe in an invisible sky daddy, as long as the big sky daddy doesn't tell them to fuck with me. If they think sky daddy has instructed them to come fuck with me, well then, we have a problem on our hands.

Ultimately, we only have each other and that the sooner we realize that, the better off we will be. I love my brothers and sisters, the human beings. Christianity is nonsense and it is holding us back. The same can be said for most other religions, with two obvious exceptions being Buddhism and Jainism.

The true creator is beyond our limited minds. We are born with a one-way radio in our minds from our creator, which is our conscience. He or she or it doesn't give us much to go on. Most of us realize that we're supposed to do good things and not do bad things. Some people listen. Some people don't. No one knows what happens after death and anyone who says that they do are simply lying. The true creator, by my best estimation, wants us to love each other and work together, and abandon ignorant concepts like racism and other irrational hatred. The sooner society can accept serious spiritual truths like these, the sooner a happy human race will arrive.

Think about this for a long while if you are a believer: Do you really, really think that there's an invisible sky daddy? If so, he's a sick fuck.

I was an atheist in the foxhole. Don't let anyone tell you that they don't exist.

Why do miracles no longer happen now that we have the technology to film them and prove their authenticity? Is it because we are sinning or that the bible is a bunch of bullshit...?

Individual beliefs are fine, but organized religion is like a virus that takes over your mind, not letting you think for yourself, but only for the spread of the virus. Upon society, it resembles a cancer. The vast majority of our populace is inflicted with religion.

I have witnessed people accepting false beliefs to get them through a difficult situation, and I'm happy that they get through it, but sometimes that false belief becomes something to cling to. If I really care about the person, I just let it slide. Why burden them with a truth that they are too weak to accept?

Our attempt to describe the divine defiles it and we place our human limitations upon it.

Your conscience is a one-way radio from the creator. Ignore it at your peril. That it is as far as religion should go and no further.

Religion is a contagious form of insanity.

The only reason children need to go to church is for indoctrination and that's a very bad reason.

Your whole life, your mind is wrapping itself around the riddle that is life. Some get closer than others. Christians are out of the race, as are Muslims and Talmudic Jews. We'd all be way better off, just listening to our hearts and ignoring alleged authorities of religion, because they are simply lying.

Excuse me Christians (and other theists for that matter) if your god is so damned awesome and real and powerful and loving, why doesn't he hang out with us so there's no doubt about his existence? You clearly have an imaginary friend.

Organized religion demands that you cease to think for yourself.

I do not deny the existence of a profound creator. I deny man's interpretation of both the creator and most descriptions of what our creator desires.

General religion is a collection of primitive belief systems.

Genitalia mutilation exists because of organized religion. That says plenty about it.

Okay, we have this really, really racist and misogynistic book that some superstitious men from the past that lived in tents wrote, that's supposed to be a guidebook to life, although it says all kinds of horrible insanity, but anyway, then they added a "New Testament" that allegedly makes all the nonsense in the "Old Testament" somehow okay. Stop me if I have confused you. Then they made up more stupid ass rules about eating Christ whenever he comes back as crackers and drinking his blood that is now wine. By the way, the church needs your money. God needs money. He created everything except apparently money...

Christianity encourages suppression of sexuality, which is bizarre and leads to horrible consequences like priests raping children, etc.

Hey religious people, check this out, I have noticed that the last two New Year's that some of you decided that the world was going to end. If you feel this way again, go ahead and leave your property to me. Think of it as a test of your faith.

If your god hates all of the same people that you do, I suspect that your god is a figment of your imagination.

Be wary of people who would cast judgment on

you because you do not adhere to their primitive belief system.

I don't deny God, I very much believe in Spinoza's god, as did Einstein. I deny a Christian god. Once we start trying to define the infinite with our limited minds, we lose sight of its profound truth and apply to it our petty prejudices. The best than we can do is listen to our conscience and act upon the principles it gives us. "I really like to think of god as the laws of physics." Carl Sagan.

Faith is the opposite of reason.

SHEEP

There is no one less free than the slave that is incapable of understanding that he exists in a condition of servitude. He will rage against you for your effort to free him. It's like corralling a hurt, scared dog that doesn't know you, to a safe place.

The uneducated; the willfully ignorant, they are as much to blame for our enslavement as those who exploit us.

Almost everything that the vast majority of people consider reality is a carefully crafted illusion. Worse still, if you try to rouse them from their slumber, they will lash out at you blindly, in defense of their servitude.

Those able to think are both feared and hated by the masses, even as those same people try to lead the masses to freedom.

The apathy of our fellow man is a large part of the reason for our servitude. Rouse him.

The sheep will mock you for your efforts, in their/my/your defense. They will be vitriolic in their description of you. They are as much to blame for our slavery as those who enslave us.

If you try to accomplish anything of substance in life, the mediocre will be your most enthusiastic detractors.

Mediocrity is for the complacent. The complacent will take what is given to them and lick their rulers' hands as would a cow its master.

Those who continually make bad decisions and cuss life for the natural repercussions of said bad decisions, well, they bother me.

I metaphorically piss in the face of the politically naive, of the willful ignorant, literally if I get the chance ... as they clearly love to have piss running down their faces.

Mediocre minds are easy to manipulate. Our oppressors rely on them.

Public schools are obedient sheep factories. If you can, home school your children.

If you perceive political reality in a "conservatives versus liberals" context, your mind is controlled by the system. Your ignorant obedience to this horrific system empowers our masters, who are no better than us and are really worse. The left/right paradigm is a false dichotomy used to keep us blinded from political reality.

A knee-jerk reaction to protect the status quo question at hand identifies gullible servants of our oppressors. BAAAH!!

It astounds me every time I realize that most people live in a delusional propaganda fantasyland, cheering for those who enslave them, which I experience on a regular basis. I always feel better as I watch the same type people start to wake up. There's not only hope, but true freedom is imminent. The powers that be fear the horrible storm that is upon them. Today's sheep may well be tomorrow's freedom warrior.

The general populace only has a vague notion of something wrong with the world as it is, but more and more are starting to see the invisible walls and realizing the systemic oppression of humanity, and they are getting angry and organizing. I love them for that.

While I disparage the sheep, we need them, at least those that can wake up and become our troops, soldiers for truth, freedom, and justice.

MISCELLANEOUS OBSERVATIONS

It will be very nice when the whole world is free and that is coming up very soon. We, as a species, are going to slam our oppressors down on the ground and erase them from existence. The war they started, they are unprepared for.

Society at large is moving forward and casting off its restraints. We have already won in the future.

Guns are freedom. If you don't own at least one gun, you're not totally free.

You are oppressed. You are a slave. I am oppressed. I am a slave. Our parents and your children are oppressed, and they are slaves, however, if enough slaves pull their minds away from the things that control their minds, and realize they are slaves, the next day there will be freedom, just like that.

Poverty is the cruelest invention ever devised by man.

Our current monetary system is nothing more than feudal serfdom in disguise.

It is said that corporations are "artificial persons" but it is more realistic to say that they are artificial sociopaths.

Your mind is the most powerful weapon that you have in your possession.

Present day economics. The bank lends you three eggs that you need to survive. You have to pay them back 4 eggs. They own all the chickens. If you're late, you owe them 7 eggs.

The value of dignity is only experienced by those who have had to demand it.

Civil disobedience is a burden of a free man.

The only guarantee in life is death. Everything else you have to take from it.

Blind obedience is intellectual cowardice.

Every difficulty is simply a situation to overcome. Each one is an opportunity to become a better person.

The big world dominating banks lend almost all of the nations of the world their currency, plus interest, which they created out of thin air. Hence, there is much more debt in the world, than currency to pay for it. Life is hard because of the parasites that make us experience pain so that they may live like gods. We all suffer but them. My people are the human beings, and that includes everyone who is not involved in holding us down. The countries that don't utilize their services; our country invades them and some of our poor people kill some of their poor people to ensure that there will continue to be poor people.

Laws and freedom have an inverse relationship.

A freedom for some, at the expense of others, is a horrible doppelganger of freedom.

The greatest war ever, may be "The Currency War". There have been precursors which all failed and those who organized them were punished horribly. The precursor wars had a very limited amount of the population aware of political realities and 100% of the media was controlled. The equation is new, and the odds favor us this time. They are powerful through an illusion. We are many because of mathematics itself.

There's a reason that we equate police officers with swine. Both are mammals that are intelligent for mammals, although less intelligent than human beings. Both are ruthless and both wallow in shit. We execute and eat one of them. I'm leaving it at that.

The problem is not overpopulation but misallocation of resources. Under population is more likely considering current reproduction rates.

Make them illegal and there will be gun cartels.

Isn't it ironically amusing that the police view themselves as "the good guys", in a sad pathetic way for society as a whole?

The Republicrat, SocialistCapitalists will solve nothing, as their very being is used to confound you. Step away from the picture which has been presented to you and ask, "What is truth?" ...and "What can I do to make the world a better place?" Then act on your best ideas.

Currency manipulation is a crime against humanity and should be treated as such.

War has been declared on the common man, by those who oppress us. It is not enough that they have enslaved us for generations, now they want 100% control. Their aspirations have outgrown our tolerance. It is now time to rise up and destroy them and all evidence that they ever existed. Oblivion is their deserved destiny.

Suppression of the truth can very easily turn into a crime against humanity. The lines are being drawn.

Righteous anger is a beautiful force.

The major revolution, which the whole world will experience in the next few years, stands a chance of being a non-violent revolution. It could seriously go either way, so prepare for some shit.

Pain is the currency with which we pay for strength.

The common man has no idea of the brute force which keeps him down. He only unknowingly experiences it, so far anyway. He's going to be really pissed when he finds out the truth.

Everybody involved in current day "capitalism", which it is not by definition, other than those who pervertedly gain from it, is upset. It's going to go down just like this, even though the bad guys are making big time plans to stay in power...once enough of our people, the human beings, wake up, there will be a tipping point which evil cannot only prevent, but will be crushed out of existence by.

There is by far more debt in the world than money and this is by design.

Small scale farming is the future. Start planting vegetable gardens and plant fruit trees and learn to preserve what you grow.

Money in our current society is control. It is

enslavement. Money is just paper that justifies our owners' sick desires. There is no stopping the opposition of our current money system. My brothers and sisters are awakening, and they are sick of the yoke of slavery that has been placed on us all. An armed populace is a free populace.

Early into the Egyptian revolution, when it became apparent that the people were going to win, the dominant controllers of that society (the Zionists) sent manned vehicles to plow into crowds of people. That is what we are dealing with. Cowards and monsters at the same time. They have no concept of a level playing field. There lies their Achilles' tendon. We have no fear of conflict. They have created an underclass that only understands conflict and therein lies their doom.

The worst criminals in the world run society and own almost everything (that they stole).

Society itself is being dismantled in front of us, because the ruling class wants one really big win, after fucking the rest of us for centuries. How bold, I'd almost salute their audacity, except for the fact that they are getting phenomenally rich, by letting our infrastructure rot and be dangerous, and Detroit is the canary in the coalmine for everyone else in the country. Things will have to get terrible before things get better.

A Few Words from, To, and About "The Man"

The Man may as well put out an instruction manual called, "Understanding Your Slavery". It might even make it easier for him.

From "Understanding Your Slavery": You are not free. You never were. You were born into bondage. Slavery has evolved to such a degree that you are likely unaware of your servitude. This is the deal. You are cattle that we, "The Man" profit upon. Some call us racists/fascists/usurers. It does not matter. You suffer the fate that we decide. You are unorganized, much like literal cattle, and we will feast upon you like we have throughout history on your ancestors, unless you wake up as a single race of human beings ... and destroy us all.

"Criticism of television is anti-Semitism!" The Man.

"Attention citizens: do not think for yourselves. We are sincerely looking out for your best interests ... bitches... " The Man.

"TELEVISION! GO WATCH YOUR TELEVISION!" The Man.

The Man's boot will not be pulled off from our throats until we flip him off by his ankles and break both his legs. Between you and me, we can do that.

"TRUTH IS AGAINST THE LAW!!!" The Man.

"If you are unhappy with your slavery, we will brand you a malcontent and a CONSPIRACY THEORIST!!!" The Man. "You may be shunned by your peers and we will actively work to make that so."

"We experience neither honor nor principles and use your inherent goodness against you." The Man.

"Be a good consumer!" The Man ...

"This sacrifice that we're asking you to make is for your benefit." The Man.

A few words about "the man": The man is on trial. He has been charged with insidious racism and wanton disregard for the good of mankind. Other offenses include crimes against humanity, human rights abuses, genocide, and economic warfare. Justice will be served.

To the Man: ATTENTION! The crowds will only continue to grow. Fuck you. We will be oppressed no more. Your doom is at hand.

PERSONAL CONDUCT AND VIRTUE

If you are without strength of character enough to protect those weaker than yourself, you are without strength of character.

Cowardice veiled by anonymity is cowardice multiplied; Loss by virtue of cowardice is loss magnified.

There is no higher truth than that found in pain. How you decide to deal with your painful experiences defines you. That is how you define yourself. Choose strength.

The advanced human being lives by his own code of ethics, which he has arrived at after great study and without influence of the common man, the sociopaths which rule us, or organized religion.

I don't appreciate the boot that has been on my neck since birth. I don't know how others don't notice it. I'll do anything to remove it, even sacrifice my life, as long as it is off my neck.

The two greatest skills in your possession are perception and reaction. You have almost absolute control of both.

Cultivate a higher morality based on what you know to be true in your heart. Live by it. There is nothing better.

It's your extreme experiences that define you; those and your reactions to them, your reactions being the more important.

Personal trauma, if correctly utilized, turns into valuable callouses for you heart, your mind, and your soul. They allow you to move forward, unafraid. Conversely it can destroy you. Choose wisely.

When you master state change, you master 90% of what it is to be a human being. Almost everyone is a slave to their emotions. When you put yourself in the driver's seat of your own mind, almost anything is possible.

The mother of all freedom is a sense of injustice by the victim, which in turn evolves into righteous indignation and finally grows into rage.

If you are forced into a violent conflict, my best advice is to recognize it and not deny it. Attack first, hit hard and focus on vital areas. When your thumb is jammed down your adversary's eye socket, he will comply with your demands. Adopt sheer brutality and use it when necessary, without hesitation.

Fearlessness is the most important attribute for a man to develop. Fearlessness does not imply absence of fear, but rather the ability to override that fear and stomp the fuck out of everyone that is causing the situation at hand.

Your decision making process should continue to improve over the course of your life.

I have very little use for, or patience with, the psychologically impotent, adult male human. Why did he not choose manhood? However, I would never victimize him.

Only accept freedom or death. I see no reconciliation occurring between those who enslave us, and us. They will not simply release us from bondage because we ask it of them. It is time that we cease being their stooges and cannon fodder. I am willing, however, to be cannon fodder in the fight to destroy them.

Buy guns, ammo, and seeds, and anything else you feel might continue your life. These are dangerous times.

Ammo not only slays your enemies but could be very useful to barter.

Those who betray their principles, reap the hopelessness that they have sown.

Personal ethics and principles should be honed and adhered to for the whole of one's life.

Defect of character disgusts me. Diligently weed them out.

There are certain behaviors that are so abhorrent to the standard agreement of what is acceptable that justify immediate execution of the guilty party, for the good of society as a whole.

Life has beating you down is unimportant. Nothing is more important that how many times you stood back up, dusted yourself off, and moved forward.

Anymore, while my initial reaction to adversity is still rage, when my mind takes over, I smile because adversity is to be embraced, as it forges us, if we let it.

The law attempts justice. A noble heart secures it.

I appreciate the law as an instrument of justice

but feel that not only does it fail that description on a regular basis, but it is oft times a tool of oppression. To run counter to the law in the name of justice; to go around the law; to go over the law, to serve what we all know is right in our hearts, is, to me, honorable and courageous.

You are the ultimate product that you will ever create.

It is a higher evolved morality which one comes to by oneself, after sincere thought, than one that is thrust upon us by an outside agency.

If you fail to prepare your children for intense, violent situations, you fail as a parent and leave them to be victimized. At a minimum, have them trained in martial arts.

Actively, and aggressively, engage in behaviors which further your best interests, relentlessly.

Hatred is a powerful force that generally produces negative repercussions to society, but when you're on the right side, and you are doing no wrong, but you keep getting beat down by an unfair system, it becomes a force for good. It becomes a superpower.

In life it is best to be passive. The wannabe badass has a terrible life. It is best to be passive until it is time to be aggressive. When that time comes, there is no other correct action except for traumatizing violence on your part, against those who do not understand. Destroy them and then be passive again. Cultivate this.

Debt is a horrible, impersonal master. Don't be its slave.

There is a huge difference between an outlaw and a criminal.

I don't like the unsavory characters that are attracted to law enforcement. They crave a badge to be able to push people around. If I wanted to push people around, I'd just push them around. I don't need a badge for that. That being said, I have very little desire to push anyone around, except assholes. Unfortunately, a lot of assholes have badges.

If you are a man, you live by your principles, ergo if you deviate from them, you are not a man.

Train your body. Train your mind. This is not a world that forgives weakness. Train your children to continue the habit.

Rage is the most logical response to injustice. Cultivate your rage as you would do a garden.

Life is actually kind of simple while it is capable of being infinitely complex. You were most likely born with a conscience. Listen to that, it's a one-way direct radio from the creator. Some people were born without that radio, and they need to be disposed of, quickly and without apology. Karma is real but does not exist for sociopaths (those without the radio that get to flourish). Those who don't understand what they are doing is wrong, are impervious to Karma. They need to be removed from this existence.

If you have not cultivated both psychological and emotional callouses, you are an incomplete human being. It's not necessary to experience trauma, but at least push yourself. Put yourself through some shit, i.e. join the military, stay in shape, train to fight, undertake things which will challenge you. Take a really stressful job for a while. Prison would make the list, but it's a bad idea to go to prison. Do things which demand mental strength. Cultivate strength and the callouses will come.

Passive resistance is just low level violence. Sometimes the right thing to do is step up the effort.

A firm system of beliefs regarding right and wrong, truth and justice, will not spontaneously exist. You will have to toil to understand why it is necessary to cultivate that part of your mind, and to forge your beliefs, but that experience will not have been wasted. Be a superior human.

Some people straight out tell you of their bad

intentions for you and present it as if it behooves you, and often their victims are bewildered, and then victimized by them. Don't be fooled. When adversaries knock on your front door, kick them head first, off from your porch, after you have beat them mercilessly; they have come to do the same to you. Some governmental agencies will do the same and should be dealt with in the same manner.

If you have no compassion for the weak, you are not strong.

Grow beyond your circumstance.

Why do so many people in this life choose victimization when an equivalent amount of emotions will slay their oppressor?

Your mind is your navigating instrument for reality. Most surrender to the reality that has been imposed upon them, but if you grab a hold of the steering wheel, very little is impossible for you; you will fear nothing and dictate your own fate. Take charge.

There are two unfortunate truths about being a truth seeker, aka, a conspiracy theorist. The first sad truth is that most people that you know are unable to process the information you are presenting them with. The other is that in your so-called camp, there are some serious nut-jobs. Nothing is more important than truth, however, continue your journey.

I see no higher virtue than dogged persistence of acquisition of truth and the dispensation of justice.

There is no acceptable excuse for failing to be the most amazing version of yourself that you can be. Focus your efforts in that direction.

I have very little patience for the cruel, for those who would gladly subjugate their fellow man, and I am capable of atrocities. Righteous indignation is a powerful force.

You cannot fully see the truth until you are jaded. Emotional callouses correct your perspective.

Does anyone out there not understand the power of validation? If you care about someone and value their presence in your life, do not fail to express that to them.

Get high and play with your cat. Go play ball with your dogs. Have both and maintain a vegetable garden.

Only the psychotic are born without fear. All emotions serve you if you are in the driver's seat of your mind.

Practice brutal honesty. Accept and encourage brutal honesty.

To be serene in the midst of chaos is the ultimate grace.

Be proud to be what you are, but also be something amazing.

If you have frustration in your life, it needs to be dealt with. Do what you have to do. Remove it, and its causes, like a surgeon would a cancerous mass with a scalpel.

Your friends are like a garden. It has to be tended to. Weeds have to be eliminated and good plants have to be nourished.

Your mind is yours to manipulate. Most are slaves to their minds. Program yours to make you a legend. It's a good idea to explore hard drugs, but then come back.

Always be prepared to accept that you are wrong, no matter how serious the contention. Apologize if you were wrong. Cultivate that. Teach that.

Be destroyed by nothing but nature and the course of time and fight those two tooth and nail.

Strive for tenacious veracity.

What is freedom, if not the ability to express oneself? That is the essence of freedom and there are forces at work to remove that ability. Vigorously oppose those forces.

The limitations which you have placed on yourself are mostly artificial and removable

Get angry and get organized.

The only adequate criteria for judging your friends, is their loyalty to you. Be loyal to your friends.

Magnify yourself.

Be determined. Be resolute. Identify your goals and chase after them, doggedly and relentlessly.

In a post-apocalyptic world, the man who can supply whiskey will do just fine as long as he has the means of production and the means to protect his product.

The two greatest skills in your possession are perception and reaction. You have almost total control of both

Imagine living your ultimate fantasy and then place your life in order to achieve those aims.

There is very little hope for the inarticulate. It is incredibly important to be an effective communicator. Make sure you have that covered.

STOP PARTICIPATING IN TELEVISION!!!

That we can stand up and admit when we are wrong; that we can accept that perhaps our truths are more fluid than we'd like to admit, make a free society available. The current powers can't do that and they have to go.

Reminisce and be grateful for your hard times. They matter most because they crafted who you are. They still do. Reminisce and be grateful for your good times. They are your reward for your hard times.

Very clearly define what is acceptable and what is unacceptable and broadcast that to society at large.

Forward your objectives. Further your cause. Advance what you believe to be correct, relentlessly. We are one people, fighting a common enemy, and we will win.

THE REVOLUTION OF HUMANITY

There is inevitably a major revolution approaching the human species. Those on top, who have parasitically prospered by our continued victimization are making plans that include nullifying the Constitution of the United States of America, and they have bought enough hollow tip bullets to kill every man, woman, and child in this country, four times over. That's scary, but they are playing by antiquated rules. They will be destroyed, and we will be free. The whole world will be free.

I'm leaving out a specific timeframe, but I will forecast long and say that the human beings of this world will join up as one and overthrow those who enslave us, who have always enslaved us, and whose comeuppance is due.

Prepare for hell itself. Hope it doesn't come to that but prepare because it may.

We, the awakened, hereby accept the war which was started by those who oppress us. We have already won in the future, and there are more of us every day. Our numbers are rising exponentially, and our enemy's numbers are miniscule by comparison.

Young male humans of the world, you have two choices: live as a coward or be prepared to die as a man.

Oppression provides the fuel for its own destruction: righteous indignation will make us all free. We have the numbers. There is ultimately no stopping us. We have already won in the future.

There is no controlling a galvanized populace.

Utilize media as a weapon against "the Man" at every opportunity. Change media into our weapon instead of a weapon used against us.

The major revolution which the whole world will experience soon, stands a chance of being a non-violent revolution, but prepare for anything.

Exploit every single weakness that the system has. Attack it. Make those in charge of it feel vulnerable. Move forward. Destroy them. Move forward.

Young men have spirit. There's a reason society uses them to fight wars. Life has not ground them down yet. It will be the younger generation, those in their late teens and early twenties now that will decide the future. They are very educated in the state of the world because they have been raised with internet. They are young and have spirit.

The revolution has already started. Prepare for interesting times.

Get angry and organize.

We will ultimately be one collective boot, stomping down on the cockroaches that currently hold us down.

The revolution of the human beings may well be a revolution of consciousness; so many of us will have awakened as to cause a tipping point which will destroy those who oppress us and simultaneously give us our freedom ... or it might be horrifically violent. Either way, it's coming sure as the sunrise. "Prepare for the worst and hope for the best."

It is time for a huge change for humanity. This change is as inevitable as the sunrise. The sun might not rise tomorrow, but I'd gladly bet my life against someone else's, that it will.

The people have already won in the future. The events unfolding will eclipse any in history.

EPILOGUE

The people that rule us are not subject to anything near application of law which we experience. They created the abnormal stress that is prevalent in society as a means of control. Be angry with them. Organize. Take action. The time is at hand for justice to finally prevail and the people to finally be free.

Also by J.D. Bradley:

Coming soon, A Dark Corner of Paradise (Poetry, Prose, and Musings from the Periphery of the Human Experience

Please visit: jdbradley.com for various writings and consider signing up there for occasional updates and you're certainly welcome to like the J.D. Bradley Facebook page. I can be reached at jdbradleyauthor-@gmail.com

And at least for the next year I have a podcast at https://www.blubrry.com/bradleyrants/ https://www.bitchute.com/channel/T5C6f6gTfAOn/ and on YouTube, just search "J.D. Bradley"

BOOKS BY THIS AUTHOR

Surreality: Strange Tales Of A Man Sitting Down The Bar From You

Review
KIRKUS REVIEW A gritty collection of true-life stories featuring themes of retribution and comeuppance.
As the subtitle suggests, Bradley, writes in a conversational, no-nonsense style that fits the raunchy content of the anecdotes in this slim, autobiographical volume. After a few tales from childhood and adolescence, he turns to his experiences in the U.S. Army, which he characterizes in retrospect as "brutal idiocy." Gleefully leaving the military behind, he settled first in Walla Walla, Washington, then in Corpus Christi, Texas. Throughout the text, the author demonstrates a low tolerance for bullies of many stripes. Whether he's targeting a corrupt police officer, a cruel military superior, or a serial rapist, Bradley... dispenses his own brand of justice and imparts cutting nuggets of wisdom:

"Place blame on life and see if it cares or stand up and be a survivor. F*ck being a victim of circumstance." Over the course of 44 brief chapters, he displays for readers a curious combination of bravado and humility, and ultimately a growing maturity. He discovered a sense of family among people who showed him compassion when he was down and out--battling depression, substance abuse, and dire economic straits. Those people included Wild Bill, a Vietnam veteran fighting cancer; Wheelchair Mike, a homeless paraplegic; and the denizens of Sweet Lips, a topless bar... Not every chapter fires on all cylinders in terms of emotional impact. However, there are enough that do for the book to warrant a look, particularly by readers with strong constitutions who can stomach large doses of reality. A work by a down-to-earth writer who tells it like it is, even when life seems harsh, unfair, or downright bizarre.

On Street Fighting: Lessons Learned In A Violent Subculture

For years I was a violent sociopath as a direct result of my childhood and then experiences as a soldier. My adventures in the methamphetamine culture certainly exacerbated that. I am not proud of this. I'm just saying what it is; that being said, this book will articulate that experience in a series of amusing anecdotes and thoughts that explain the important lessons that I learned during that time; lessons I learned with contusions, abrasions, a couple of lacerations, my own blood, some jail time, a lot of craziness, and a great deal of pain.I highly recommend this book for martial artists, as their training does not cover, or even understand, the social dynamics of violence, aspiring street fighters that will gain a great deal of real world knowledge on this subject, anyone interested or fascinated by violence and/or fringe subcultures, and any fan of Taratino movies and/or Bukowski writing. Nothing like this has every been written before.You will learn how to substantially damage other people with some of this knowledge, among other things. I do not recommend this lifestyle and am no longer part of it, but I also regret nothing.This book is for educational purposes only. Neither the author nor the publisher assumes any responsibility for the use or misuse of the information contained in this book. Fighting is both dangerous and illegal.

www.ingramcontent.com/pod-product-compliance
Lightning Source LLC
Chambersburg PA
CBHW072051040426
42447CB00012BB/3090

* 9 7 8 0 9 8 8 8 1 8 0 0 2 *